I0440964

SMAÏN and SAFTI'S SUMMER DAY

Robert Hichens

[ZHINGOORA BOOKS]

This edition is published by
Zhingoora Books.

Apart from any fair dealing for the purposes of research or private study, or criti-cism or review, this publication may only be reproduced, stored or transmitted, in any form or by any means, with the prior permission in writing of the publishers. All disputes are subject to exclusive jurisdiction of Mandsaur Courts only. For any suggestions and feedback or book on new concept/domain, please contact us at the email given below.

contact@Zhingoora.com

Contents

SMAÏN

"When the African is in love he plays upon the pipe."

Sahara Saying.

Far away in the desert I heard the sound of a flute, pure sound in the pure air, delicate, sometimes almost comic with the comicality of a child who bends women to kisses and to nonsense-words. We had passed through the sandstorm, Safti and I, over the wastes of saltpetre, and come into a land of palm gardens where there was almost breathless calm. The feet of the camels paddled over the soft brown earth of the narrow alleys between the brown earth walls, and we looked down to right and left into the shady enclosed spaces, seamed with water rills, dotted with little pools of pale yellow water, and saw always giant palms, with wrinkled trunks and tufted, deep green foliage, brooding in their squadrons over the dimness they had made. The activity of man might be discerned here in the regularity of the artificial rills, the ordered placing of the trees, each of which, too, stood on its oval hump. But no man was seen; no flat-roofed huts appeared; no robe, pale blue or white, fluttered among the shadows; no dog blinked in the golden patches of the sun—only the sound of the flute came to us from some hidden place ceaselessly, wild and romantic, full of an odd coquetry, and of an absurdity that was both uncivilised and touching.

I stopped to listen, and looked round, searching the vistas between the palms.

"Where does it come from?" I asked of Safti.

His one eye blinked languidly.

"From some gardener among the trees. All who dwell in Sidi-Matou are gardeners."

The persistent flute gave forth a shower of notes that were like drops of water flung softly in our faces.

"He is in love," added Safti with a slight yawn.

"How do you know?"

"When the African is in love he plays upon the pipe. That is what they say in the Sahara."

"And you think he is alone under some palm-tree playing for himself?"

"Yes; he is quite alone. If he is much in love he will play all day, and, perhaps, all night too."

"But she cannot hear him."

"That does not matter. He plays for his own heart, and his own heart can hear."

I listened. Since Safti had spoken the music meant more to me. I tried to read the player's heart in the endless song it made. Trills, twitterings, grace notes, little runs upward ending in the air—surely it was a boy's heart, and not unhappy.

"It is coming nearer," I said.

"Yes. Ah, it is Smaïn!"

Safti's one eye is sharp. I had seen no one. But as he spoke a tall youth in a single white garment glided into my view, his eyes bent down, his brown fingers fluttering on a long reed flute covered with red arabesques. His feet were bare, and he moved slowly.

Safti hailed him with the accented violence peculiar to the Arabs. He stopped playing, looked, and smiled all over his young face. In a moment he was on our side of the earth wall, and talking busily, staring at me the while with unabashed curiosity. For few strangers come to Sidi-Amrane, and Smaïn had never wandered far.

"What does he say?" I asked of Safti.

"I tell him we shall be at Touggourt tomorrow night, and shall stay there a week. He answers that his heart is there with Oreïda."

"What! Does his lady-love live at Touggourt?"

"Yes; she is a dancer."

Smaïn smiled. He did not understand French, but he knew we were speaking of his love affair, and he was not afflicted with shyness. As he accompanied us to the village he played again, and I read his nature in the soft sounds of his flute.

All that day he stayed with us, and nearly all that day he played. Even when he guided me through the village, where, between terraced houses, pretty children—the girls in deep purple, with yellow flowers stuck in their left nostrils, the boys in white—danced with a boisterous grace round brushwood fires, his flute was at his lips, and his fingers fluttered ceaselessly. And as night drew on the music was surely more amorous, and I seemed to see Oreïda drawing near over the sands.

Smaïn was but sixteen, tall and slim as a reed, with a poetic face and lustrous, languid eyes. I imagined Oreïda a child too—one of those flowers of the desert that blossom early and fade ere noontide comes. Sometimes such flowers are very beautiful. As I heard the flute of Smaïn in the pale yellow twilight I knew that Oreïda was beautiful—with one of those exquisite, lithe figures, whose movements make a song; with long, narrow dark eyes, mysterious pools of light and shadow; with thick hair falling loosely round a low, broad forehead; and perfect little hands, made for the dance of the hands that the Bedouin loves so well.

All this I knew from the sound of Smain's flute. I told it to Safti, and bade him ask Smaïn if it were not true.

Smain's reply was:—

"She is more beautiful than that; she is like the young gazelle, and like the first day after the fast of Ramadan."

Then he played once more while the moon rose over the palm gardens, and Safti, lighting his pipe of keef with tender deliberateness, remarked placidly:

"He would like to come with us to Touggourt and to die there at Oreïda's feet, but his father, Said-ben-Kouïdar, wishes him to remain at Sidi-Matou and to pack dates. He is young, and must obey. Therefore he is sad."

The smoke rose up in a cloud round Smaïn and his flute, and now I thought that, indeed, there was a wild pathos in the music. The moon went up the sky, and threw silver on the palms. The gay cries from the village died down. The gardeners lay upon the earth divans under the palmwood roofs, and slept. And at last Smaïn bade us good-bye. I saw his white figure glide across the great open space that the moon made white as it was. And when the shadows took him I still heard the faint sound of his flute, calling to his heart and to the distant Oreïda through the magical stillness of the night.

The next day we reached Touggourt, and in the evening I went with Safti and the Caïd of the Nomads to the great café of the dancers in the outskirts of the town. At the door Arab soldiers were lounging. The pipes squealed within like souls in torment. In the square bonfires were blazing fiercely, and the whole desert seemed to throb with beaten drums. Within the café was a crowd of Arabs, real nomads, some in rags, some richly dressed, all gravely attentive to the dancers, who entered from a court on the left, round which their rooms were built in terraces, and danced in pairs between the broad divans.

"Tell me when Oreïda comes," I said to Safti, while the Caïd spread forth his ample skirts, and turned a cigarette in his immense black fingers.

The dancers came and went. They were amazing trollops, painted until, like the picture of Balzac's madman, they were chaotic, a mere mess of frantic colours. Not for these, I thought, did Smaïn play his flute. The time wore on. I grew drowsy in the keef-laden air, despite the incessant uproar of the pipes. Suddenly I started—Safti had touched me.

"There is Oreïda, Sidi."

I looked, and saw a lonely dancer entering from the court, large, weary, crowned with gold, tufted with feathers, wrinkled, with greedy, fatigued eyes, and hands painted blood-red. She was like an idol in its dotage. Over her spreading bosom streamed multitudes of golden coins, and many jewels shone upon her wrists, her arms, her withered neck. She advanced slowly, as if bored, until she was in the midst of the crowd. Then she wriggled, stretched forth her hands, slowly stamped her feet, and promenaded to and fro, occasionally revolving like a child's top that is on the verge of "running down."

"That is not Oreïda," I said to Safti, smiling at his absurd mistake. For this was the oldest and ugliest dancer of them all.

"Indeed, Sidi, it is. Ask the Caïd."

I asked that enormous potentate, who was devouring the withered lady with his eyes. He wagged his head in assent. Just then the dancer paused before us, and thrusting forward her greasy forehead, enveloped us with a sphinx-like smirk. As I hastily pressed a two-franc piece above her eyebrows Safti addressed her animatedly in Arabic. I caught the word "Smaïn." The lady smiled, and made a guttural reply; then, with a somnolent wink at me, she waddled onward, flapping the blood-red hands and stamping heavily upon the earthen floor.

"Smaïn loves that!" I said to Safti.

"Yes, Sidi. Oreïda is famous, and very rich. She has houses and many palm-trees, and she is much respected by the other dancers."

A week later Safti and I were again at Sidi-Matou, on our way homeward through the desert. The moon was at the full now, and when we rode up to the Bordj the open space in front of it, between us and the village, was flooded with delicate light. Against it one tree, which looked like Paderewski grown very old, stood up with tousled branches. In the village bonfires flared, and the dark figures of skipping children passed and re-passed before them. We heard youthful cries echoing across the sands. Soon they faded. The lights went out, and the wonderful silence of night in the desert came in to its heritage.

I sat on the edge of an old stone well before the Bordj, while Safti smoked his keef. Near midnight, quivering across the sands, came the faint sound of a flute moving from the village towards the deep obscurity of the palm gardens. I knew that air, those trills, those little runs, those grace notes.

"It is Smaïn," I said to Safti.

"Yes, Sidi. He will play all night alone among the palms. He is in love."

"But with Oreïda! Is it possible?"

"Did he not say that she was like the first day after the fast of Ramadan? When an African says that his heart is big with love."

The flute went on and on, and I said to myself and to the moon, as I had often said before:

"He that is born in the Sahara is an impenetrable mystery."

SAFTI'S SUMMER DAY.

By Robert Hichens

Safti is a respectable, one-eyed married man who lives in a brown earth house in the Sahara Desert. He has a wife and five children, and in winter he works for his living and theirs. When the morning dawns, and the great red sun rises above the rim of the wide and wonderful land which is the only land that Safti knows, he wraps his white burnous around him, pulls his hood up over his closely-shaven head, rolls and lights his cigarette, and sets forth to his equivalent of an office. This is the white arcade of a hotel where unbelieving dogs of travellers come in winter. I am an unbelieving dog of a traveller, and I come there in winter, and Safti comes there for me. I, in fact, am Safti's profession. Byrne, and others like me, he lives. For a consideration he shows me round the market, which I knew by heart six years ago, and takes me up the mosque tower, from which I gazed over the flying pigeons and the swaying palms when Safti was comparatively young and frisky. Together we visit the gazelles in their pretty garden, and the Caïd's Mill, from which one sees the pink and purple mountains of the Aures. We ride to the Sulphur Baths, we drive to Sidi-Okba. We take our *déjeuner* out to the yellow sand dunes, and we sip our coffee among the keef smokers in Hadj's painted café. We listen to the songs of the negro troubadour, and we smile at Algia's dancing when the silver moon comes up and the Kabyle dogs round the nomads' tents begin their serenades. And then I give Safti five francs and my blessing, and he bids me "*Bonne nuit!*" and his ghostly figure is lost in the black shadows of the palm-trees.

Oh, Safti works hard, very hard in winter. The other day I asked him: "Don't you get exhausted, Safti, with all this exertion to keep the Sahara home together? You are getting on in years now."

"Ah yes, Sidi; I am already thirty-two, alas!"

He was thirty-five when I first met him; but he is as clever at subtraction as a London beauty.

"Good heavens! So much! But, then, how can you keep up the wear and tear of this tumultuous life? You must have an iron strength. Such work as you do would break down an American millionaire."

Safti raised his one dark eye piously towards Allah's dwelling.

"Sidi, I must labour for my children. But in the summer, when you and all the travellers are gone from the Sahara to your fogs and the darkness of your days, I take my little holiday."

"Your holiday! But is it long enough?"

"It lasts for only five months, Sidi; but it is enough for me. I am strong as the lion."

I gazed at him with an admiration I could not repress. There was, indeed, something of the hero about this simple-minded Saharaman. We were at the edge of the oasis, in a remote place looking towards the quivering mirage which guards dead Okba's tomb. A tiny earthen house, with a flat terrace ending in the jagged bank of the Oued Biskra, was crouched here in the shade. From it emerged a pleasant scent of coffee. Suddenly Safti's bare legs began to "give." I felt it would be cruel to push on farther. We entered the house, seated ourselves luxuriously upon a baked divan of mud, set our slippers on a reed mat, rolled our cigarettes, and commanded our coffee. When a Kabyle boy with a rosebud stuck under his turban had brought it languidly, I said to Safti:

"And now, Safti, tell me how you pass your little holiday."

Safti smiled gently in his beard. He was glad to have this moment of repose.

"Each day is like its brother, Sidi," he responded, gazing out through the low doorway to the shimmering Sahara.

"Then tell me how you pass a summer day."

The coffee nerved him to this stubborn exertion, and he spoke.

"*Sahah* Sidi."

"*Merci.*"

We sipped.

"A day in summer, Sidi, when the great heats begin in June? Well, at five in the morning I get up——'

"And light the fire," I murmured mechanically.

The one eye stared in blank amazement.

"Proceed, Safti. You get up at five. That is very early."

"The sun rises at a quarter to five."

"To call you. Well?"

"I eat three fresh figs, and sometimes four. I then mount upon my mule, and I ride very quietly into Biskra to take coffee with my friends."

"That is half-an-hour's exercise?"

"About half-an-hour. After taking coffee with my friends we play at dominoes. It is forbidden for the Arabs to play at cards in Biskra. I remain in the café at the corner—"

"I know—by the Garden of the Gazelles!" "—till eleven o'clock, at which time I again mount upon my mule, and return quietly to my home. When I reach there I eat with my wife and children sour milk, bread, and dates from my palm-trees which I have kept from the autumn. At twelve we all go to bed together in a black room."

"A black room?"

"We fear the flies."

"I see."

"Till four in the afternoon I, my wife, and my children sleep in the black room. At that hour I rise once more, and go quietly to the Café Maure in old Biskra, near my house. I play cards there for five coffees till seven o'clock. At seven the mosquitoes arrive, and prevent us from playing any more."

"How intrusive! Always at seven?"

"Always at seven. I then walk very quietly with my friends to the end of the oasis."

"To the Tombuctou road?"

"Yes, Sidi; to get the air. We come back by the same road quietly, and I go to my house, and eat a cold kous-kous with my wife and children. After this I return to the café and play ronda till one o'clock."

"One o'clock at night?"

"Yes. At one o'clock I go with my friends very quietly to bathe in the stream beneath the wall near the mosque. We stay in the water for, perhaps, an hour, and when we come out we drink lagmi."

"What's lagmi?"

"Palm wine. Then at three o'clock I go to my home, mount upon the roof quietly with my wife and children, and sleep till dawn."

"And you do this for five months?"

"For five months, Sidi."

"And—and your wife, Safti?"

I felt that I was very indiscreet; but Safti is good-natured, and has bought quite a number of palm-trees out of his savings when with me.

"My wife, Sidi?"

"What does she do all the time?"

"She remains quietly in my house."

"She never goes out?"

"Never, except upon the roof to take a little air."

"Doesn't she get rather bor———"

The one eye began to look remarkably vague.

"And you find five months of this life a sufficient rest in the course of the year?"

Safti smiled at me with resignation.

"I cannot take more, Sidi; I am not a rich Englishman."

"Well, Safti, you must make the best of your fate. It is the will of Allah that you should toil."

"*Shal-làh!* I will take another coffee, Sidi."

"Larbi!"

I called the Kabyle boy.

End of the book.

www.ingramcontent.com/pod-product-compliance
Lightning Source LLC
Chambersburg PA
CBHW071349310526
45790CB00018B/1400